STICKS AND STONES
Life Lessons From a Lawyer

by Theresa A. Lyons, Esq.

PANAM BOOKS
Where Words Take Flight

Published by

PanAm Books
P. O. Box 3179
Upper Montclair, NJ 07043
www.panambooks.com

Permissions on file for use of Trade Name:
"Bobbleheads."
Other Trade Name/Trademark usage: Permissions Pending.

ISBN-13: 978-1-942693-13-0

ISBN ebook-13: 978-1-942693-14-7

Sticks and Stones, Life Lessons From a Lawyer
Library of Congress Control Number Available

PRINTED IN THE UNITED STATES OF AMERICA

Cover and Interior Design by McB Design

PROLOGUE

What does a lawyer know about life? On most days, not much.

But every once in a while, the law, just like life, provides us opportunities for growth—teachable moments, reasons to look twice.

The legal stories in this book are happy, and tragic, and funny, and strange. Some stories are deeply disturbing. And the reason for such a hodgepodge is because the law itself is a reflection of life. Much of what we experience as humans—the good, the bad, the ugly, the weird—also exists within the law. The Justice System is not some foreign object up high in the sky. It is an everyday thing run by everyday people.

When reading this book of legal stories, I ask you to be open. Let yourself laugh, and cry, and think, and feel. Most important, however, be open to the many life lessons that wait to be learned.

CHAPTER 1

LIFE LESSONS *FROM* A LAWYER
Sticks and Stones
May Break My Bones ...

Family #1:

A New Jersey couple had three children and named them as follows: Adolf Hitler, Aryan Nation, and Honszlynn Hinler.

The family first came to the attention of the general public when the parents went to a local grocery store to have a birthday cake made for their son. They wanted to order a cake that bore a Swastika and said "Happy Birthday Adolf Hitler." The worker behind the bakery counter refused to fill the order. Insulted by such disrespect, the parents took their outrage to a local newspaper and complained that their rights of free speech were being violated.

When the story hit the news, child protection services became involved. They found Nazi paraphernalia and decorations adorning the family home. New allegations arose, including a substantial history of domestic violence in the home, and that one of the children was being taught how to kill.

The parents did not understand why child protection services removed custody of their children and started litigating against them. Nor did the parents understand why the judge ultimately decided to terminate their parental rights, even though the father wore his Nazi uniform to the final day of court.

Family #2:

A lawyer was headed to court on a typical Wednesday morning for a typical case management conference. What was not typical, however, was that the night before, the lawyer had suffered a horrific root canal and spent three hours in the dentist's chair. The lawyer could not eat dinner on Tuesday night, or breakfast on Wednesday morning, but off to court she dutifully went.

While sitting in court awaiting her turn to see the judge on what was otherwise a routine day, and with her stomach growling with hunger pains, the lawyer watched the following divorce being held on the record in open court:

Judge: Mr. Hamburger, are you ready to proceed?

Husband: Yes.

Judge: Mrs. Hamburger, are you ready to proceed?

Wife: Yes.

Judge: Very well. Mr. Mark Hamburger was married to Mrs. Susan Hamburger on February 23, 1997, in a religious ceremony. They have three children together: Thomas Hamburger, born December 16, 1998, Dylan Hamburger, born June 23, 2001, and Janice Hamburger, born September 6, 2004....

☀ LIFE LESSON:
... and sometimes names <u>can</u> hurt me.

*According to press reports, although the New Jersey grocery store would not help the parents with their Nazi birthday cake, a store in Pennsylvania did. If you owned a bakery, what would you have done? Why?

One Man's Trash Is Another Man's Treasure

There was a neighborhood that stood amidst time-entrenched poverty and up-and-coming gentrification. Within that space existed a cyber café. It had big cushy seats and featured fashionable overhead lighting. Patrons munched on foods with hip names like "byte-size cookies" and sipped on extra-caffeinated beverages called "re-boot" while listening to the latest new-age-elevator-music-type songs as they streamed through hidden speakers.

Much like other businesses caught on the cusp between the haves and have nots, there were times that the café's patrons felt uncomfortable entering the place because of the homeless people, drug addicts, and beggars roaming the street in front. (One reason why there were so many homeless people roaming the street in question is because of a shelter and counseling center located nearby.) After a while, cyber café patrons could be heard remarking that they needed to leave at earlier hours so as not to encounter too many miscreants on the way home.

The owner of the café complained to the police and thought the authorities were not doing enough to keep the "bad people" away. He also approached the executive director of the homeless shelter and asked for help. When the director of the shelter told the cyber café owner to "sign off," it was the final straw. The owner instituted a law suit against the shelter for its refusal to control its clientele, alleging that the shelter and its indecents "prohibited the progression of honest business development."

News of the suit hit local newspapers, and the clash of the classes was on.

Just as homeless people often do, and in response to the suit, they took to the trash cans—the café's trash cans. Along the way, the homeless people discovered some not-so-decent tax information about the café's owner, which had inadvertently been discarded.

The homeless people brought the information to the authorities. The lawsuit ended quickly.

☀ LIFE LESSON:
People in glass houses shouldn't throw stones.

Have you ever walked by a homeless person rummaging through the trash? What thoughts went through your mind when you saw that person? Most likely, you didn't think that he or she was conducting legal research for a court case, but at the end of the day, we never really know how or why any person arrives at his or her set of circumstances, and we also never really know how or why a particular person is motivated to do what he or she does. Things are not always as they seem, and no book or person should ever be judged by its cover. (Except to the extent that maybe the cover on this book made you buy it—then it is ok for you to judge a book by its cover, but otherwise, don't do it again in the future.)

Smile and Say "Cheese"

Carol was a woman who was fighting for custody of her three teenage children. In getting ready for trial, she brought pictures to her lawyer's office that showed her and the children sitting in the living room of her apartment opening Christmas presents, and playing board games together, and engaging in other types of fun activities that families often do. The photographs all showed a clean home that was nicely decorated, with art on the walls, plenty of school pictures, and a lovely small plant on the side coffee table.

At the custody trial in court, Carol's lawyer introduced the pictures. First, he meticulously asked the court clerk to mark each picture for identification. Next, he had Carol verify the authenticity of each picture and name all the people in them. Then, the lawyer had each picture entered into evidence one by one as part of the official court record. After all of that, it was time for cross-examination by Carol's husband's lawyer. This is how it went:

Lawyer: Ma'am, these are lovely pictures of you and your children. Do all of these pictures accurately depict your living room as it exists on a regular everyday basis when you and your kids are home?

Carol: Well, yes, except the Christmas tree in that one. We don't always have that in my living room every day.

Lawyer: Of course not, forgive me Ma'am. But the rest of your living room, when it is not the holidays, is that how your apartment usually looks when you and the kids are home?

Carol: Most of the time, yes.

Lawyer: Isn't it true Ma'am, that in these pictures, the plant on your side coffee table is a cannabis plant?

Carol did not win custody.

≊ LIFE LESSON:
A picture is worth a thousand words.

How do you think Carol's lawyer felt? Yes, in some ways, losing custody was Carol's fault, but it was her lawyer who was so caught up in the litigation, and who was so focused on the process of marking and identifying the pictures, that he failed to see the small, yet deadly detail of the cannabis plant. Many times in life, we too overlook the small details. Often it is the small details that tell the real story of what is going on. The next time you find yourself in an otherwise mundane situation, look for the small details—the proverbial plant on the side table. You might just be surprised by what you ultimately find.

Good Fences Make Good Neighbors

Victoria was a victim of domestic violence for many years. Her husband, George, would beat her repeatedly for all kinds of reasons: not having dinner ready, wearing the wrong outfit, and failing to complete certain tasks around the house. Victoria was not allowed to work outside the home. She was given no financial control and was not permitted to socialize with any of her friends or extended family.

One Thursday, George came home, saw that the lawn had not been mowed, and proceeded to beat Victoria black and blue. The next morning, George left for work. Victoria went outside to hang some laundry (the dryer had broken the week before, but Victoria was afraid to tell George about it for fear of repercussions). Her face was black and blue as she lay George's clothes across the line. Victoria's next door neighbor, Sam, saw her from afar and walked over to say hi. Sam was a handsome and gentle soul who lived with his elderly mother and worked nights at a local hospital. Truth be told, Sam had a secret crush on Victoria for a while, but being the gentleman that he was, Sam would never think of acting on it.

When Sam saw Victoria's face, he asked her what happened. "I fell down the stairs and hit my face by accident." Sam didn't believe her, so he pressed her for answers. Eventually, Victoria broke down. She told Sam what was happening and how everything was her fault, "I should have known better than to put the lawn off. George works so hard."

Sam tried to convince Victoria that she was not to blame, that George's actions were not ok, and that she should consider getting some help. "You are very kind," Victoria said, "but really, this is my problem, not yours." Victoria then rushed back inside.

The following Thursday morning, after George left for work, Victoria heard the faint sound of a lawn mower. She looked out her window to see Sam mowing his own grass. He had always done such a good job. Victoria admired the efforts for a few seconds, and then she went back to her kitchen duties. A few minutes later, the sound of the mower grew closer. She looked out her window again, and there was Sam mowing her grass too. Victoria ran from the house and up to Sam, "Why are you doing this?" Sam responded, "I don't want George beating you up about something as stupid as grass. Honestly, he shouldn't be beating you up about anything. But if you won't take my other advice, at least let me do this for you." Victoria nodded shyly, and went back inside. In fact, Victoria was starting to have a little secret crush on Sam as well, but she would never act on it either because, in her mind, no man like that would ever want someone like her.

Sam's work continued for the rest of the summer. Every Thursday morning, without fail, he mowed Victoria's lawn. One day in late August, George unexpectedly came home from work while Sam was mowing. George had forgotten something that he needed for a meeting at work. When George pulled into his driveway, he saw Sam mowing. George politely waived and said, "Thank you." George left home without incident to go back to the office. Later that night, Victoria was beaten senselessly because, in George's mind, she must have been doing something slutty in return for Sam's kindness. As part of the struggle, George slammed Victoria's head against their bedroom dresser, shattering her eye socket. Blood poured out.

Victoria could take no more. She called 9-1-1. The police came and took George away, and an ambulance brought Victoria to the hospital. Besides her shattered eye socket, Victoria also suffered a broken nose. She required a protective face mask and was scheduled for a series of surgeries. She also received counseling from a women's group, and filed for a Temporary Restraining Order that night by speaking with an emergent duty municipal judge over the phone. Because of the severity of the injuries, the women's group was able to arrange for Victoria to get a free lawyer to go to court to try to help her convert the Temporary Restraining Order into a permanent one. On the day of the trial, Sam drove Victoria to court. He sat with her in the back of the courtroom and promised to keep her safe. An advocate from the women's group also came to court that day to lend Victoria emotional support.

George arrived and walked into court. Victoria was sitting with Sam, the lawyer, and the advocate. She started to sob at the sight of George, and the tears dripped through the wire holding the facemask together. Her nose ran, but because of the mask, she could not even properly wipe her face. Victoria's lawyer whispered, "It's ok. He can't hurt you here." Victoria responded. "No, that's not it. I love him so much. George needs me. I know that by being here, I am doing the wrong thing."

Against the advice of her attorney, and over the recommendations of the victim advocate from the women's group, Victoria dismissed her restraining order. She left court with George that day. Sam left alone. Sam never mowed her lawn again.

🜂 LIFE LESSON:
Sometimes the grass is greener on the other side.

Statistically it takes the average victim of domestic violence seven attempts to successfully leave her abuser. Statistics also show that the most dangerous time for a victim of domestic violence is immediately after trying to leave the relationship. Why do you think that Victoria didn't choose to leave George? Are there any legitimate reasons for her (or other people in Victoria's situation) to stay? How did her decision make you feel? Would you feel differently if they had children together? How do you think Victoria's lawyer felt when he was standing at counsel table next to her as she dismissed her restraining order in open court? Finally, it should be noted that, if you are wondering what happened to Victoria after she went back to George, and you want to know whether she is ok today, you are not alone. The lawyer never heard from Victoria again either, which makes the lawyer just like you—forever condemned to wonder. The law (like life) does not always give closure.

A Sign of The Times

Story #1:
Legend has it that a disgruntled Wife bought this billboard for a period of six months.

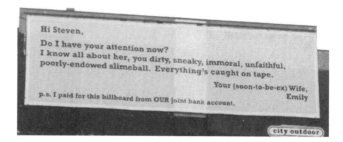

Hi Steven,

Do I have your attention now?
I know all about her, you dirty, sneaky, immoral, unfaithful, poorly-endowed slimeball. Everything's caught on tape.

Your (soon-to-be-ex) Wife,
Emily

p.s. I paid for this billboard from OUR joint bank account.

city outdoor

Legend also has it that Steven's divorce attorneys were able to make sure that Emily could not pay for the billboard entirely out of marital savings. So, that was a win. But a legend isn't a legend without some type of anguish. For reasons of free speech, and because there was no last name on the sign, the judge ruled that the sign could not be removed until the contract was over. So for six months every morning, Steven and his co-workers—one of whom happened to be the person who was having the affair with the "dirty, sneaky, immoral, unfaithful, poorly-endowed slime ball"—had the privilege of reading that sign on the way into work.

Story #2:
Helen and Jeff lived together for a number of years, and things began to get boring. In order to spice things up, they decided to invite another woman into their bed and into their relationship.

The threesome enjoyed six full months of wild and interesting sex. Over the course of that six months, a funny thing began to happen. Jeff started to fall for the other woman. But so did Helen. And when Helen realized that the other woman was starting to have feelings for Jeff rather than for her, she became jealous and filed fake domestic assault charges to get Jeff kicked out of the apartment. Jeff had to hire a lawyer and faced an eleven day trial just to get back into his apartment.

Eventually, all allegations were dismissed, and Jeff did get back into his apartment, but not before he incurred $18,300 in legal fees.

☀ LIFE LESSON:
The law be damned, hell hath no fury like a woman scorned.

Here Rover ... Good Boy!

Two brothers owned houses that were right next door to each other. Aiden was the older brother, and he had a dog. His younger brother, Billy, hated that dog.

Aiden worked the early shift at the factory, and he had to report to work each morning at 6:00 a.m. Because of that, every day at 5:30 a.m., Aiden would let his dog into the back yard, and then leave for the day.

The dog liked to bark—a lot. From the moment Aiden pulled out of his driveway, that dog barked, and howled, and made all kinds of other loud noises that were very disturbing to Billy.

Billy tried to complain to Aiden, but Aiden would have none of it and could not believe that his beloved best friend was really causing that much harm.

In order to prove his case, Billy thought of

a good idea. One day after Aiden left for work, Billy snuck onto his property and planted a video recorder to capture the mayhem. When Aiden got home from work, Billy showed him the video tape and tried to speak to him again, still with no luck.

So Billy decided to file a formal lawsuit, and this is what he claimed: a) harassment; b) negligent infliction of emotional distress; and c) civil violation of a local ordinance prohibiting noise pollution. Billy asked for $25,000 in damages.

When Aiden received the lawsuit, he decided to counter-sue, and this is what he claimed: a) violation of privacy for planting the video camera on his property without permission; b) harassment; and c) defamation of character. He too sought $25,000 in damages.

When the case went to trial, Billy's case was thrown out. He received no money for the barking dog. However, Aiden did win on the violation of privacy claim. He was awarded $25,000.

☀ LIFE LESSON:
Let sleeping dogs lie.

Many people go to court without considering all of the costs. And there are many costs when going to court: financial, emotional, time, and energy. Legal shows on TV don't reveal all the costs of going to court. Everything looks so glamorous, and all problems are usually wrapped up in 60 minutes or less, even with the commercial breaks. A good lawyer will discuss with his or her client all the financial costs of going to court. A great lawyer will discuss with his or her client not just the financial costs, but the emotional and many other costs as well.

Sign Right Here on the Dotted Line

Stan met Christine at a bar, and within six days, they fell madly in love. They immediately set the wedding date, and church bells could be heard pealing in the distance. Because Christine's family had some rather large assets, everyone agreed that a prenuptial agreement was necessary.

Stan sent over the first draft of what he wanted Christine to sign. Most of the prenuptial agreement contained the standard language addressing property and assets, but there were two sections of the proposed agreement that really caught Christine's eye. They read like this:

SECTION 3.7: Sexual Intimacy. Both parties recognize the important role that sexual intimacy plays in a happy marriage. Accordingly, upon marriage,

Wife shall put forth her best efforts to keep the parties' romance alive. To that end, Wife shall present herself to Husband for sexual intimacy at least twice each month in newly purchased lingerie, said lingerie to be selected by Wife but paid for by Husband. In the event that Wife fails to present herself to Husband for sexual intimacy in lingerie at least twice per month, then Husband shall have no obligation to pay for any of Wife's other clothing expenses.

SECTION 3.8: Physical Appearance. Because of the importance of sexual intimacy as expressed herein at SECTION 3.7, Wife acknowledges and accepts her responsibility to keep her own physical appearance as attractive as possible. Wife shall not be required to undergo plastic surgery. However, Wife warrants that she shall not gain more than 10 pounds above her weight as of the date of the execution of this agreement, except during pregnancy. In the event that Wife becomes pregnant, she shall have up to 180 days after the end of her pregnancy to get her weight back to within 10 pounds of her weight as of the date of this agreement. Husband shall pay all expenses necessary at the gym of Wife's choosing in order to assist her in fulfilling her responsibility under the terms of this agreement.

Christine decided not to sign the agreement. She also decided not to marry Stan.

☀ LIFE LESSON:
"Caveat emptor"—let the buyer beware.

*Often when we begin a new relationship (personal, professional, or otherwise), we start by thinking about what we want to get from it and what we want the other person to give us. We rarely think about what the other person might be looking for from us, and more importantly, whether we really want to give what they are seeking. In your next new relationship, whatever kind it might be, think twice not just about what you want, but also about

whether you are willing and able to give what the other person wants as well. If you are not willing and able to give what is sought, that is ok, and it may be better to admit that fact sooner rather than later. Up front honesty tends to save a lot of time, energy, and aggravation down the road.

Divorce Account #1:

Nancy had a wicked nasty divorce. It took four and a half years to complete. She burned through every liquid asset she had. She lost her house. Her kids needed therapy. She was so consumed by the vitriol that she even got fired from her job because she could not focus on her career. By the time the divorce was over, she already had paid her attorney $210,000, and she owed another $173,000 in unpaid fees.

Two weeks after her divorce was final, Nancy dropped dead of a sudden heart attack. Her attorney sued the estate and collected every penny of the remaining $173,000 from a life insurance policy that was payable to Nancy's estate.

Divorce Account #2:

Tom and his wife separated amicably ten years ago.   They never went to court; they never fought about anything; they never wasted any time or any money. They each simply went their separate ways.

After ten years of being happily and peacefully separated, Tom decided it probably was time to get formally divorced. So, with his separated-wife's permission, Tom went and hired a lawyer. He paid a retainer of $5,000, and he asked the lawyer to file very friendly no-fault divorce papers. Tom called his wife on the way home from the lawyer's office to let her know that he had just hired a lawyer. Tom's wife agreed it was time, and filing the papers was the right thing to do.

Three days after paying the $5,000 retainer, and before the no-fault divorce papers were filed, Tom choked on a piece of pizza and died. The lawyer kept the retainer.

Divorce Account #3:

Fred and John were a same sex couple that lived together for 26 years and entered into a

Civil Union. After Fred found John cheating on him with their strapping young pool boy, Fred filed for dissolution of the Civil Union, and the couple litigated the matter for two years. On the day of their supposed trial, all matters were settled, and the couple hoped to avoid further legal costs by just putting their dissolution through as an "uncontested" matter.

However, right before the couple was to go in front of the judge, John suddenly remembered that the couple owned adjoining cemetery plots in San Francisco. The couple had pre-purchased the plots in the earlier days of their marital bliss. Now that they were about to get divorced, neither party wanted to spend the rest of eternity buried next to the other, but neither party wanted to let the other one buy him out either. (Apparently, they were very nice elevated plots on a rolling hill overlooking a calm landscape with a grove of lovely flowering trees.) The adjoining burial plots had to be addressed.

The total combined value of the plots was $12,700. The parties spent the next three days in court, for eight hours each day, fighting over the grave plots. John's lawyer charged $390.00 per hour. Fred's lawyer charged $425.00 per hour. The total fees incurred on that issue alone were $19,560. At the end of three days of fighting, the judge threw up her hands and ordered the plots to be sold, and the money was used to pay the lawyers' fees. Neither Fred nor John got the prized land.

☀ LIFE LESSON:
No matter how or when you die, the lawyer always gets paid.

CHAPTER 2

LIFE LESSONS *FOR* A LAWYER (And All Professionals)

According to Merriam-Webster, the definition of being a professional means, "relating to a job that requires special education, training, or skill." But how about this for a definition instead? Being professional means that you keep plugging away and doing what you do, even when it sucks.

Every professional faces a moment of truth when he or she struggles and realizes that they can't fix everything that they were originally trained to fix. Think of the doctor or nurse whose patient unexpectedly dies, or the teacher who loses a student to the streets, or the lawyer who realizes that justice is not always that just.

And when that crisis hits, the real professional will experience three things. First, there is disbelief—the thought that "this can't be happening." Then there is disillusion—the sadness, the anger, the questioning, "Why should I keep trying so hard?" Finally, there is action on one of two paths: the professional will either choose to leave the profession (literally or by way of emotional apathy), or the professional will resign himself to keep doing what he originally set out to do with continued passion and vigor, knowing full well that he cannot save everyone. She cannot always get it right. He likely will fail again. Defeat will happen, and it will happen more than once. That is the moment of proof.

This section of the book is devoted to all those professionals who keep plugging along with passion, who keep being human, and who keep fighting the good fight, even when it sucks.

Only The Good Die Young

Todd is a disgusting man. He and his wife, Cheryl, had a little girl. From the time that little girl was just nine months old, Todd performed hard core acts of repeated anal and vaginal intercourse upon his young infant daughter.

As the small child grew and began to try to resist, Cheryl would hold the child down to permit her husband to mount and thrust.

When the child was four years old, she herself tried to mount another child in her preschool class. When the teacher pulled the child aside to find out how and where she learned such acts, all came to know.

Todd and Cheryl were arrested. Todd showed no remorse. He bragged and laughed about the fact that his daughter's first word was "fuck"—not mommy, not daddy—but "fuck."

Todd was charged with numerous criminal counts that, if convicted of, would have put him in jail for life.

The child was placed with extended relatives out of state. When it came time for Todd's trial on child rape and all of the other multiple criminal charges he faced, the new caregivers, the teachers, and all the mental health professionals agreed that if there was a long criminal trial, the required testimony would be too traumatizing for the small, healing, yet still fragile girl.

For that reason, and that reason only, Todd was offered a plea deal. Rather than being sentenced to life in prison for multiple counts of child rape and sexual assault, Todd instead was permitted to plea to the lesser infraction of child endangerment. He received a sentence of only six years.

Todd spent the entirety of his six year sentence filing appeals to the various courts as to why he should be released early and why he should not have been sentenced for six years. The government spent thousands of dollars on his case between the pre-trial work, the plea, and the numerous appeals.

☀ LIFE LESSON:
Some people shouldn't have children.

Do you think it was easy for the lawyers involved in the matter? Imagine that you were one of the lawyers who was assigned to work on this case—which competing interest would have been more important to you: punishing Todd or protecting the little girl from having to testify in court? Did the justice system get it wrong for not putting Todd in jail long enough? Did it do the right thing by helping the little girl move on with her life more quickly? In the justice system, in corporate America (and life in general), we often face situations where the "right" answer is not so obvious. True professionals grapple with the fact that most decisions are not black and white. And ironically, the graver the dilemma, the more likely it is that the decisional lines become blurred. To be human means to face crisis without clear cut certainty.

I'll Be Home For Christmas

Gerry was 72 years old. He loved two things more than life itself: his grandchildren and good scotch, lots of it.

After spending his life drinking too much, he developed liver disease. He spiraled downhill over a period of four long years, and his loving grandchildren watched as Gerry slowly developed all kinds of hideous symptoms. He suffered jaundice, anemia, distention, and polydypsia and polyuria (excessive thirst and excessive, frequent urination).

On December 22, Gerry went to see his regular doctor who discovered that, because of his excessive drinking and his recent weight gain that put him into the obesity category, Gerry also had developed high blood pressure. So, the doctor prescribed a very basic medication to try to address his blood pressure.

Gerry went home that day, after stopping at a local bar for some semi-good scotch. (Gerry could not afford his regular good scotch that day because of the co-pay he had just rendered to his doctor, so instead he was forced to settle for the lower quality.)

On December 23, Gerry went to his local drug store and filled his new prescription. On the way home, he stopped at another local bar for good measure and good scotch. (This time, he did splurge.)

On December 24, at 6:53 p.m., Gerry and his family were enjoying a lovely Christmas Eve dinner. It was snowing outside, and all the world was at peace. Gerry's wife was clearing the table from dinner and asked Gerry to carry a bag of garbage out to the can. Gerry agreed. Halfway down the sidewalk, Gerry suddenly collapsed into a state of unconsciousness. His wife screamed, and everyone ran outside. Gerry lay there still, with the snow falling about him, as his sobbing grandchildren shook him and whispered, "Grandpa, Grandpa. Please don't die on Christmas."

Grandpa died on Christmas.

Gerry's family sued the pharmaceutical company that manufactured the blood pressure medication, saying that the medication caused Gerry to have an embolism. They demanded a payment of $120,000.

The pharmaceutical company had very high-priced lawyers and the best medical experts on the planet. They were confident they could show a jury that Gerry died from complications of his liver disease, his obesity, and his alcoholism, rather than from side effects from the blood pressure medication. The company rejected all settlement talks.

The jury entered an award of $3.7 million against the pharmaceutical company. Gerry's family bought a lot of good scotch that day.

☀ LIFE LESSON:
Often it's better to take your losses than to take your chances.

*Have you ever heard someone say, "It's the principle that matters"? In this case, the pharmaceutical company and its lawyers were extremely confident because they knew they were "in the right."

They very well may have been "in the right," but their principled beliefs did not carry the day. Principles are important things. In many ways, they define us as human beings. But every principle has certain costs and risks. Understanding those costs and risks, and being able to put them into perspective when needed, is just as important as having the principles themselves.

When It Rains It Pours

Michael was convicted of a double murder he didn't commit. At age 27, he was sentenced to serve life in prison without parole. Michael went to jail for a very long time.

When Michael was 61 years old, new evidence came to light. The prosecutor was forced to admit that the original conviction was wrong. Michael was a free man, an old man, but a free man nonetheless.

Less than 48 hours after being released from prison, Michael suffered a stroke. Michael is now paralyzed. He traded the confines of iron bars for the confines of an iron chair.

☀ LIFE LESSON:
Bad things do happen to good people.

Possession is 9/10 of The Law

Scenario #1:

A well-known professional athlete had left many of his childhood belongings at his parents' home—high school jerseys, rec-league trophies, old sneakers, and the like. His mother took possession of those items and tried to sell them through a high-end auction house without her son's permission. The professional athlete sued his mother, and litigation began. Eventually, the parties settled the matter. Mom got to sell some things, but not all.

Scenario #2:

The following is a list of items that were dropped off at a local attorney's office for safekeeping. Some of these items were deposited at the lawyer's office per court order. Some items were dropped off because clients thought the items would be helpful to their cases. Some items were simply dropped off because clients wanted assurances that their belongings would be held without harm.

- Red Porsche
- BB gun air rifle
- Philly Fanatic costume
- Nude photos
- Smart phone
- Jewelry
- Pet remains (thankfully in an urn)
- Dishes
- Passports
- Sex tapes – audio and video
- Prescription drugs
- Diary
- Empty vodka bottles
- Disney Christmas ornaments
- Broken computer
- George Bush Bobblehead (not "W" – the other one)
- Guitar
- Used underwear
- Brooks Brothers' Suit
- Wedding photo album

- Bottle of wine (1978 Montrachet)
- Human sperm in a Ziploc baggie
- Prosthetic arm
- Section of a roof from a battery manufacturing company

☀ LIFE LESSON:
The best things in life (or in Court cases) aren't necessarily things.

There is no class in law school that teaches lawyers how to handle people's "stuff" (physical, emotional, otherwise). Yet, every day, lawyers are charged with just that—helping to decide what to do with, and how to handle, people's stuff. If, due to life circumstances, your possessions were in danger of being lost, and you could bring just one of your belongings to a lawyer's office for safe keeping, what would you bring and why?

SMART PHONES, DUMB PEOPLE

Russell's girlfriend, Evelyn, filed a Temporary Restraining Order against him. As part of her complaint to the court, Evelyn alleged harassment, and she predicated her claim on the fact that Russell continued to send her over 30 text messages a day—even though she repeatedly asked him to stop contacting her.

However, there was one small problem. Evelyn herself was also sending Russell text messages—about 40 a day. But because the judge did not know that on the first day that Evelyn went to court, she was successful in getting the Temporary Restraining Order put into place. Russell was served with the official papers, and the matter was set down for a full trial eight days later.

As part of the Temporary Restraining Order, Russell was completely prohibited from having any contact with Evelyn or any members of her family. If he violated the Temporary Restraining Order and tried to contact her in any way, he would instantly be arrested.

Russell knew he had to hire a lawyer to protect himself. So, he asked around and was able to find the top lawyer in town. Russell paid an up front retainer of $2,000 just to be able to have the first meeting at the lawyer's office.

During the meeting, Russell told the lawyer about all of the daily text messages that Evelyn kept sending. The lawyer was excited because he thought that perhaps the text messages could help Russell's defense. So, the lawyer asked to see Russell's cell phone in order to examine the text messages and to determine whether they could, in fact, be used against Evelyn at trial.

The lawyer was able to retrieve Evelyn's text messages. For sure, they were very helpful for Russell's case. However, while the lawyer was scrolling through the text messages, he accidentally hit the "contact" button, and the phone instantly called Evelyn. Panicked, the lawyer quickly hung up, but it was too late. Evelyn saw the missed call from Russell, she called the police, and a warrant was then issued for Russell's arrest.

Embarrassed and feeling guilty, the lawyer accompanied Russell down the police station to try to defend him through the arrest process. The lawyer sheepishly had to admit to the police and to the emergent on-duty judge that it was he, not Russell, who accidentally dialed Evelyn. Luckily, Russell was never criminally prosecuted for the violation.

🔔 LIFE LESSON:
Technology sucks.

Have you ever accidentally "butt dialed" someone? Did you ever receive an e-mail scam? Have you ever accidentally sent the wrong text message to the wrong person? Technology has improved our lives in many ways. But just like other tools harnessed by humanity (think nuclear science), technology has the power for good and for evil. Technology's biggest strengths—ease of use, speed of trans-mission, availability to the masses—are also its greatest weaknesses. Be careful how you use it.

Case #1:

Lawyer: I want to talk to you about the repairs needed to the marital home and how the parties are going to handle the bills.

Client: I need a restraining order.

Lawyer: Why?

Client: My husband came into the home and left me a harassing note.

Lawyer: What did the note say?

Client: He called me nothing but a horny, yapping hole.

Lawyer: Can I see the note?

Client: Sure. Here it is....

yapping hole in house. Give this to your aHorney.

Case #2:

After 23 years of marriage, Don left his wife for a woman half her age and nearly half her weight. Throughout the entire process, even though her feelings were hurt, Don's wife was still cordial, reserved, and amicable. For that reason, Don chose to proceed without hiring a lawyer. His wife did hire counsel.

Once the parties came to a settlement, Don needed to sign a document to finalize the divorce, but because he was representing himself, that document had to be signed in front of a witness. Don executed the document, had it witnessed, and dropped off the document at his wife's lawyer's office. The wife's lawyer met Don in the lobby and took the form. Although the witness' signature looked a little strange, the lawyer thought nothing of it. After all, the parties were proceeding amicably.

On the day of the parties' divorce, they both were standing in front of the judge. When the lawyer took out the signed document from Don and presented it to Don's wife to ask some questions on the record, a strange look came over her face.

That look turned from strange to rage as she exclaimed: "That's the whore! That's the whore! The witness on this paper is the bitch who broke up our family!"

The judge banged his gavel, the lawyer asked for a recess, and Don spent two hours in the hallway apologizing, while trying to convince his wife to still put the divorce through that day. The divorce did go through that day, but not until Don had to pay a little extra money to sweeten the now-stirred pot.

☀ LIFE LESSON:
Penmanship is important.

We go through our daily lives, and we forget the importance of being meticulous. Take pride in the details. It's the details that can often make or break any given situation.

He Said, She Said

Teresa and Dominick were getting divorced. They had one daughter, who was twelve years old when the divorce started.

Every chance Teresa had, she bad-mouthed Dominick to the child. "Your father is a lying, cheating asshole. Because of him, you and me are going to be penniless, and he doesn't care."

Dominick was no better. He also bad-mouthed Teresa whenever he could. "I wouldn't have left home if it weren't for your mother. She is an out of control bitch, and if you know what's good for you, you won't grow up to be anything like her."

Over the course of the litigation, Teresa and Dominick couldn't agree on a single thing about their daughter. They fought about the child's clothes, her school, her friends, and they even fought about what to buy the kid for her birthday. To make matters worse, Teresa and Dominick had all of their fights in front of their daughter.

Neither parent noticed when their daughter's grades fell, or when she began to withdraw from all of her friends. They were too busy fighting instead.

On the day before their divorce trial was supposed to begin, Teresa and Dominick each received a call from the local police. Their daughter (now fifteen years old) threw herself off a bridge on her way home from school.

Ironically, although Teresa and Dominick couldn't agree on anything else over the past three years, they were able to agree on the coffin in which their teenage daughter was buried.

🚨 LIFE LESSON:
We reap what we sow.

The Doctor Will See You Now...

Peter was a teenage boy who really loved his older sister Linda. So when Linda asked Peter to donate one of his kidneys to save her life, he was happy to oblige. He was nervous, but still willing.

Into the hospital Peter went. Linda had already been in the hospital waiting because her health was so fragile. Linda was suffering from end-stage renal failure.

The doctors brought Peter into one operating room and Linda into another, and then put them both under anesthesia. The doctors successfully removed Peter's kidney, and they carefully placed it into a container of protective bio-slush in order to transport the kidney to where Linda lay waiting.

A nurse mistakenly threw the kidney into the garbage thinking it was surgical waste.

When the other nurses realized the

mistake, they retrieved the kidney and tried with the doctors to resuscitate it, but there was nothing they could do. The donated kidney was damaged too badly, and it could not be used at all.

Peter left surgery one kidney lost, and Linda left surgery no kidney found.

The siblings sued the hospital where the transplant was to take place. They also sued the medical professionals who conducted the surgeries, including the nurse who accidentally threw the kidney away. According to court papers, Linda had to bear the continuation of painful dialysis, more surgeries, and the anguish of awaiting another kidney from someone else. Peter sued because of the painful and dangerous surgery he underwent and the fact that he now has to live the rest of his life with just one kidney—all in vain.

🔔 LIFE LESSON:
Haste makes waste—sometimes literally.

*To err is human, to sue is revenge. Or is it? Not every error is purposeful, and

not every lawsuit can right every wrong. There are situations in life when bad things happen—and no apology, no action, no system can make it right. Moreover, the "waste" is not necessarily in the haste of the initial mistake. Sometimes the waste occurs when we continue to dwell on things for which there is no real redress. It takes a strong person to be at peace with the fact that some things just can't be fixed.

Quench That Thirst

Story #1:

Jake was a teenage boy. He thought it would be a good idea to try to shake a soda vending machine in order to get some free soda and some extra spare change.

Jake's shaking of the machine got a little out of hand. Suddenly, and before Jake knew it, the machine tipped over and landed directly on top of him. With a large bang, the glass shattered, cans of soda rolled about, and multiple coins lay strewn upon the ground. Jake suffered a bruised rib and several large lacerations. Jake also was charged with the following acts:

- Criminal Mischief
- Petty Theft
- Disturbing the Peace

Jake appeared in juvenile court. He was sentenced to fifty hours of community service. Jake avoided soda machines for many years to come.

Story #2:
Antonio had a suspended driver's license. One day for the heck of it, he took a friend's car and went for a drive anyway. He ran a red light and crashed his car through the wall of a local fast food restaurant. Several customers were injured, but luckily nobody was killed—not even Antonio.

Antonio was, however, charged with the following crimes:

- Driving while having a suspended license
- Vehicular assault
- Careless driving
- Reckless endangerment
- Failure to wear a seatbelt

☀ **LIFE LESSON:**
Junk food is bad for you.

*Most lawyers have a personal vice. For some lawyers, it's junk food. For others, it's caffeine. For some, it's a good drink or an afternoon cigarette. It helps us when a case doesn't go our way, or when a client refuses to follow our advice and we know they are going to get clobbered because of it, or when we just plain get sick and tired of reading fancy Latin phrases like "ipso facto" or "ex post facto." A lawyer without a good personal vice is like peanut butter without jelly. Technically, a person can get away with making a sandwich that has either peanut butter or jelly all by itself, but it just doesn't feel complete. For any person or professional, substance falls short without a little sweetness on the side.

CHAPTER 3

There once was a court stenographer named Xavier. A court stenographer is a person that sits in court and uses a small type-writer like machine to transcribe what everyone says and does in court. The court stenographer's job is very important because, if there ever is a question about what happened in court, or if there ever is an appeal to a higher court, the only things that are considered part of the "official record" are those things that the stenographer actually writes down. If the stenographer fails to write something down, it is like it never happened.

Xavier was sick of his job. One day, he thought it would be cute to insert the phrase "All work and no play makes Jack a dull boy" into the official court transcript.

As the days passed, Xavier got even more sick of his job. So, instead of transcribing what everyone was saying in court, Xavier instead started typing, "I hate my job, I hate my job, I hate my job" over and over and over again.

It took a while for the lawyers and the people in the courthouse to discover what Xavier was doing. By the time he was caught, Xavier messed up so many transcripts that at least thirty criminal convictions had to be overturned by the State because there was no real proof as to what was said and done in court during those cases. Otherwise convicted criminals were set free.

Needless to say, Xavier no longer has to hate his job. He was fired. He (and Jack) now have plenty of time to play.

☀ LIFE LESSON:
The pen is mightier than the sword.

The courts and the justice system (like many other things in life) are only as strong as their weakest link. There are so many good and caring professionals who run the legal system. It is not just lawyers and judges. There are clerks, probation officers, *couriers, legal secretaries (there is a special place in Heaven for legal secretaries), paralegals, mail room workers, bail bondsmen, hearing officers, translators, techies, court appointed experts, sheriff's officers, and the list goes on. It is easy to forget sometimes that the justice system is actually run <u>by</u> the people <u>for</u> the people. It is not just some abstract thing up in the clouds. It is a collective and ongoing effort of purposeful individuals who really do work hard to try to get it right. And most of the time, they do.*

Lady Luck

Everybody who knew Ron saw him as a bad man. Without warning, Ron closed the local convenience store he owned, left his wife, served her with divorce papers, and let their marital home go into foreclosure. Ron refused to pay any of his wife's bills, refused to contribute towards her shelter expenses, and refused to pay any alimony. Ron was, of course, a bad man.

Ron's wife garnered sympathy from a woman's advocacy center, and she was able to obtain an otherwise very high priced lawyer on a *pro bono* (free) basis. The high priced lawyer filed a strong and quick application with the court seeking Ron's immediate arrest. The judge summoned Ron, his wife, and the high priced lawyer in for an emergency hearing, making it known in advance that the judge was thinking about having Ron arrested. After all, Ron was a bad man.

On the day of the emergent hearing, Ron arrived without counsel. The wife arrived with her high priced lawyer.

The judge quickly swore in the parties, and with a very stern voice he barked at Ron, "Sir, give me one good reason why right now I should not throw you in jail." Ron replied, "Your Honor, I am sad and ashamed to be here today. I wish I could pay my bills and take care of my wife, but she has a terrible gambling addiction."

"OBJECTION!" Exclaimed the high priced lawyer, jumping out of the chair at counsel table.

The judge responded, "I understand your concern counsel."

The high priced lawyer sat down and whispered to the wife, "Is it true what Ron says?" "NO" she replied, very emphatically and very convincingly.

Then the judge turned to Ron and asked, this time in a more tempered tone, "Why do you say that sir?"

"When I used to own the convenience

store, there was a lottery machine at the counter. My wife used to spend $400 a day on lottery tickets. Now I have multiple judgments against me from the state gaming commission and a whole bunch of other people. I have been trying to pay everyone back as best I can. I have not been making this situation public because it's totally embarrassing, not just for me as a local business owner, but also for my wife's reputation as well."

Now a little concerned about Ron's seemingly sincere tone, the high priced lawyer again whispered to the wife, "Did you ever spend $400 a day on lottery tickets?" "No" stated the wife. "That's a lie."

The high priced lawyer leapt up again: "OBJECTION!"

The judge decided to bypass the high priced lawyer and instead directly addressed the wife. "Ma'am, you heard your husband's testimony just now. What say you?"

Wife: "That's a lie. That's a lie. I never spent $400 a day in lottery tickets. The most I ever spent was only $200 a day in lottery tickets."

The judge looked at the high priced lawyer. The high priced lawyer sat down, as the many other litigants and lawyers sitting in the back of the courtroom chuckled out loud. Ron was not arrested. His wife left with no money and no prospect of future support. People who were not in court that day still see Ron as a bad man, and they cannot understand how the justice system so miserably failed his wife.

☀ LIFE LESSON:
Never gamble more than you can afford to lose.

*Oftentimes we hear about verdicts in the news, and we become upset or enraged about the outcomes. We wonder, "How could that have happened?" Or we say to ourselves, "The jury must have gotten it wrong." Ron's case is a perfect example of someone who was misjudged by the public, but at the end of the day, deserved vindication. The press and the Internet rarely tell the whole story. It usually is impossible for them to do so. Trials can

last many days and even months. Without sitting through an entire trial, without seeing all witnesses and hearing first-hand their personal stories, it is hard to know for sure whether any given outcome is just or not. The next time you find yourself questioning a verdict that you hear about in the news, take a moment to pause and ask yourself whether you really do know the whole story. Maybe something else was going on that you and the rest of the public were not aware of.

Polly Want a Cracker?

Paolo and Amelia were married near the rolling hills of Rio de Janeiro. The wedding was simple, but the rum was plentiful, and there was an endless feeling of romance in the air.

Because Paolo was a bird lover, Amelia bought him the coolest present ever on their wedding day: a rare Double Yellow-Headed Amazonian Parrot. They named him "Sempre," which translated into English means "Always" because that bird, their marriage, and the love they shared would last forever.

The couple lived together in marital bliss. Sempre learned to dance to Samba music. He even started talking, learning such phrases as "olá" (hello) and "beije me" (kiss me). Life was perfect.

Eleven years, two kids, and a heap of bills

later, Paolo and Amelia started to drift apart. One day, the family was sitting at the dinner table when Amelia's cell phone rang. Sempre called out, "Sergio." The kids laughed, Amelia apologized for having her phone near the dinner table, and Paolo shrugged it off. The next week at breakfast, Amelia's cell phone rang again. Sempre again called out, "Sergio."

Paolo became suspicious. He tracked Amelia's cell phone records and eventually learned that Amelia was having an affair with a gentleman named Sergio.

As part of the divorce, the parties fought about the kids and the bird. The judge decided that Amelia got the kids, but Paolo got to keep Sempre. The bird was, after all, a gift for always.

Unfortunately, however, old habits die hard. Every time the phone rang in Paolo's new apartment, Sempre continued to call out "Sergio." Heartbroken, Paolo donated Sempre to a local retirement community, and he never saw the bird again.

☀ LIFE LESSON:
Silence is golden.

Joe was a man saddled with a large alimony obligation of $50,000 per year, and he had about twelve years worth of payments left to make until the alimony would end. He knew his ex-wife was shacking up with another man, but had no way to prove it. The ex-wife, their friends, and even the parties' son were lying about it.

If Joe could somehow prove that his ex-wife was living with another man, he could make an application in court to end all of his alimony obligations, thereby saving himself about $600,000 worth of total payments.

So what did Joe do? He hired a private investigation firm.

The private investigators tried all kinds of tricks to try to prove the cohabitation. They conducted surveillance. They pulled phone records. They did "trash runs." Trash runs are a common practice in the industry whereby private investigators go to people's homes and steal trash from the curbs in the hopes of obtaining relevant documents or other useful information. A well-executed trash run involves several steps: 1) scoping out the residence to determine what night the trash is put out; 2) finding out what type of trash bags that home uses; 3) going back on another night to steal bags of garbage from the can on the curb; 4) replacing the stolen bag with a bogus bag of trash in a similar looking bag; and finally 5) taking the stolen bag to headquarters to examine and analyze the refuse.

Nothing worked. The ex-wife and her cohabitor were using side and back entrances to their home, were keeping very separate records, and were even shredding their garbage and taking it to large public dumpsters at their work places. The investigators could not prove what everyone knew was happening.

One day, the private investigator had a stroke of genius. The ex-wife happened to work as a manicurist at a local upscale salon—one of those frou-frou places catering to very rich women. The salon was known for serving its patrons cinnamon biscuits with organic chai tea, and also for playing only the finest classical music. What if one of the investigators posed as a client getting a manicure and then used the opportunity to gather information directly from the ex-wife by engaging her in what would otherwise seem like harmless conversation? Everything else had failed, so Joe and the private investigators decided to give it a shot. The plan was set in motion.

The investigator chosen for the job was Judy. Judy was picked because she was smart and because her undercover skills were beyond compare. However, much like Sandra Bullock in *Miss Congeniality*, Judy was not necessarily comfortable with her femininity. She had coarse hair and a slim figure that often was hidden by bulky clothes. She had never gotten a manicure in her life. And when first approached by her boss at the investigating firm, although Judy was excited about going undercover, she did not relish the thought of having to subject herself to a manicure and all of that other girly stuff that came with it.

Nevertheless, Judy went to the salon. She presented herself and asked for an appointment with the ex-wife for a manicure.

What Joe's ex-wife did not know was that Judy had planted a recording device in her newly purchased purse. (Judy also rarely carried a purse, but she had to play the part.)

Judy got her cup of gourmet chai with a lime twist and walked toward the manicure station. This is the conversation that ensued:

Ex-wife: So, have you ever had a manicure before?

Judy: No, this is my first.

Ex-wife: Great. What brings you here today?

Judy: I am going through a divorce and decided to treat myself.

Ex-wife: Oh, honey, I completely understand. I myself went through a divorce a couple of years ago and totally feel your pain. We'll have lots to talk about. Sit down and make yourself comfy.

Judy sat, and the ex-wife gave her a manicure. Frankly Judy didn't care for it, but she didn't quite hate it either, much to her surprise.

And so it was. Every Tuesday afternoon for a year, Judy went to get a manicure from the ex-wife. Sometimes it was French. Sometimes it was regular. Around the holidays, Judy would get airbrushing as well. Judy even branched out and tried an occasional cinnamon biscuit with her gourmet chai tea. Secretly, Judy began to enjoy the manicures. She looked forward to them. She actually felt kind of pretty, which was a new concept for her. Judy liked getting her nails done.

The ex-wife, not knowing Judy's real mission, began to see Judy as more than a client. She was a weekly regular, a friend, someone she could talk to. By the end of the year, the ex-wife had confided in Judy and bragged that she was living with her boyfriend, that he wanted to marry her, that she was making everyone she knew lie about it including her son, and that the sole reason why she was engaging in such deception was to keep receiving her stupid ex-husband's alimony checks for $50,000 a year. All the while, Judy's tape recorder was running in

Judy's only purse. She was getting the job done, no matter how much chai tea she had to choke down.

After all of the information was collected, Joe and his lawyers made an application to the court to terminate all alimony. As part of his application, Joe presented the court with transcripts from the conversations between the ex-wife and Judy. Joe asked for sanctions, attorney fees, and all kinds of other scary things. Joe's ex-wife caved instantly, even before the judge said a single word. Joe won. He never paid another penny in alimony again.

Once the cat was out of the bag as to how the secret information was gathered, Judy could not return to the salon. Judy never enjoyed another manicure again. She missed her weekly pampering, and was very sad, although she never could admit it, because after all, it was always just a job. Wasn't it? At least she got to keep the purse.

☀ LIFE LESSON:
At some point, beauty must give way

to substance.

Judy is a good example of how some-times lawyers and other professionals become unexpectedly changed by client interactions. We meet our clients and other people where we find them, we hear their stories, and we make assumptions as to how those stories came to be and how those stories will ultimately be resolved. Yet, along the way, there often can be opportunities for the professional to learn things about themselves as well—if they are smart enough and open enough to let it happen. True engagement is a two-way street.

If The Shoe Fits...

Mr. Clardy was a twenty-six year old pimp. When a customer of his failed to pay for the services of one of his prostitutes, he decided to take action. Using his Nike Jordan sneakers, Mr. Clardy repeatedly stomped on the customer's face, causing the customer to require many stitches and plastic surgery.

Mr. Clardy was convicted of not only assault, but also of robbing the customer and beating the prostitute as well. The prostitute's injuries were so severe that she bled from her ears. Mr. Clardy eventually was declared a "dangerous offender," and he was sentenced to one hundred years in prison, with a chance of parole after thirty-six years.

Mr. Clardy did not realize that Nike shoes were such a dangerous weapon. He went on to sue Nike, claiming that the company had "failed to warn of risk or to provide an adequate warning or instruction" that the shoes are a "potentially dangerous product." According to Mr. Clardy, Nike had the obligation to put clearer warning labels on the shoes so that others would know of the shoes' ability to cause such extensive personal injuries.

☀ LIFE LESSON:
Keep your feet on the ground.

Daddy Knows Best

Harry and his wife, Elizabeth, had one daughter. The child's name was Laura, and she was born with severe birth defects, including spina bifida and congenital heart problems. Laura spent much of her young life on feeding tubes, using breathing machines, and undergoing countless surgeries. She had trouble sleeping at night, suffered seizures, and could not control her bowels.

When Laura was just six years old, her parents got divorced. As part of the process, they had a long custody battle and a thirteen day trial. At trial, the judge was having a hard time deciding who should be awarded custody. Both parties stated their cases on the record as to why they should have Laura, and the judge listened intently. As the matter unfolded, and the judge watched more and more, he noticed a certain calmness about

Harry. He was serene; he was unruffled. And while the judge couldn't quite put his finger on it, he began to feel that Harry's sense of inner peace would make him better equipped than Elizabeth to raise Laura and to deal with the many future challenges that would be faced. It was clear that both parents loved Laura, but Harry was more up for the task.

On the final day of trial, which happened to be a Friday, the judge rendered his decision from the bench. Harry was to take custody of Laura immediately. Elizabeth was to have parenting time, to be scheduled around the child's needs and various medical appointments. Both parents were to be involved in major life decisions about Laura, but day-to-day, Harry was to raise her. Harry was happy and looked at peace. Elizabeth wept.

When the judge left the courthouse that night and started home, he re-played the entire trial over and over again in his head. He thought about each and every word the parents had said. He felt sorry for Elizabeth, but the judge also took solace in knowing that he had made the absolute right decision for the best interests of the child. Harry was the slightly better parent.

On Sunday morning, the judge was reading his newspaper and enjoying a cup of coffee when he saw the following headline:

FATHER "MERCY" KILLS DAUGHTER BY SMOTHERING IN SLEEP
Dad tells police better to die
than live with disabilities.

☁ LIFE LESSON:
Beware of a wolf in sheep's clothing.

It is not easy to be a judge. Imagine spending most of your days sitting on an elevated bench, or locked in a windowless office, physically removed from the public over whom you preside. Now imagine that you also earn less money than the average lawyer who regularly appears before you. Even though TV makes it look easy (think "The People's Court"), the truth is that most judges are over-worked and under-appreciated. The public rarely compliments judges for cases that are well-decided, but we certainly are quick to criticize if something goes wrong. And when we publicly criticize judges, the law generally prohibits them from being able to respond. They are required to keep things to themselves, no matter how painful it might feel. Judges are people too. Sometimes they get it wrong. But every judge swears a duty of allegiance to the public and its laws, and to the extent that anyone thinks that judges have an easy time laying that burden down at the end of their work day, think again. How do you think the judge felt as he walked back into the courthouse on Monday morning or the next time he had to take the bench to decide another custody matter?

Is It Better To Give Or To Receive?

Person #1:

A Virginia prison inmate named Robert Lee Brock was angry at himself for getting arrested for breaking and entering and grand larceny. This being America, the only logical thing to do was to institute a formal lawsuit against himself in Superior Court. In his complaint against himself, he alleged that he had wrongly violated his own religious beliefs by committing the crimes, and he sought payment for a civil rights offense. He asked for a payment of $5 million in damages. Since he was incarcerated at the time and had no way of paying off the $5 million judgment he sought, he asked that the State pay the money on his behalf. The suit was thrown out.

Person #2:

In 2001, a man hoping to save his marriage decided to donate his bone marrow to his ailing wife. According to a local press interview, the husband said, "My first priority was to save her life. The second bonus was to turn our marriage around."

The bone marrow procedure was very successful. The marriage, not so much.

In 2005, the man's wife cheated on him. She also slapped him with divorce papers and took custody of their kids.

Distraught, the man said, "There's no deeper pain you can ever experience than to be betrayed by the person you devoted your life to."

To help ease his sadness, the man filed a lawsuit against his wife seeking one of two things: either the return of his bone marrow, or $1.5 million—whichever was more feasible.

After some litigation, the divorce judge threw out the man's case. The judge found that, while the notion of marital property can be "expansive," it cannot and should not include human tissue or organs. The man received neither the return of his bone marrow, nor the $1.5 million. Needless to say, neither did the man enjoy the return of his wife.

Person #3:

Pam was a nice lady whose adult son, Josh, suffered from schizophrenia and Capgras delusions. (Capgras is a disorder in which a person holds a delusion that a friend, spouse, parent, or other close family member has been replaced by an identical-looking imposter.) Pam tried desperately to get Josh help from the local mental health clinic, but when that clinic failed to properly give Josh his much needed medication, he snapped. He killed Pam by stabbing her with a butcher knife. He also killed his younger brother.

Josh was found not guilty of the two murders by reason of insanity. Instead of being sent to prison, Josh was institutionalized in a mental health hospital run by the State.

Pam's estate sued the local clinic for wrongful death, claiming that, had the clinic properly treated Josh, Pam would not have been killed. Pam's estate won $800,000 in damages from the local clinic.

Josh is one of the beneficiaries of Pam's estate. He filed a lawsuit from inside the institution to collect his piece of the $800,000.

☀ LIFE LESSON:
Charity starts at home, but it does not always stay there.

Families are microcosms of the larger world. In many ways, the law and human life are influenced by all the good, bad, and ugly that emanate from the family unit. Just like it is unrealistic to expect every family to be able to cure or contain every woe, so too must we as people be mindful of our own systemic shortcomings as well. Some things still remain too complicated to wrap our minds around. Maybe that's a good thing.

Pay Day!

Story #1

Carla loved to shop, and her favorite local store was just one mile from home. She became as happy as a kid in a candy store when she heard that her favorite store was having a special: "Flavo-straws" at 88¢ a box.

Carla really wanted to load up. She went into her home supply of spending money and took out two new $100 bills that she had withdrawn from the bank about a month ago, but had been waiting to spend.

Off to the store Carla went. She loaded up her cart with "Flavo-straws." While she was there, she also picked up a giant case of paper towels, some canned cheese product, and a couple of new throw pillows.

Carla proceeded to the check out line. She happily handed her first $100 bill to the clerk to pay. The clerk, thinking the bill was counterfeit, ripped the bill in two. A manager was called over. Carla tried to explain that her $100 bill was not counterfeit, and she showed the manager her other $100 bill. The manager yanked the second $100 bill out of Carla's hand and ripped that one in half too, for the manager also thought the bills were counterfeit. Then the manager called the police and told Carla that she was not allowed to leave the store until the police arrived. Carla was mortified at the public display.

Carla sued the store for an undisclosed number of $100 bills. She claimed that the store perpetrated "intentional infliction of emotional distress and false imprisonment."

Story #2:
In 1972, John tried to rob a bank in New York City. During the attempted robbery, he kept several of the bank employees hostage for over seventeen hours.

John was captured and sent to jail, but the story was sensational. Warner Brothers made a movie about the robbery. The movie was sensational too. It was nominated for an

Academy Award.

John, feeling "exploited," started what would become forty years of litigating against the movie makers to try to collect his "fair share" of the movie proceeds.

☼ LIFE LESSON:
Money isn't everything.

While both of the above stories look on the surface like they are about money, they really are not. The true issue is the personal insult that each individual felt was suffered, and the public sense of vulnerability created therefrom. Most of the time when lawyers or other people argue about "the money," there is a deeper issue that needs to be addressed. Soothe and solve that deeper issue, and the money usually falls in to place.

Shit Happens...

A mom took her six-year-old son to a local circus for his birthday. Mom bought great seats—right in the first row—and they were both very excited to go. While at the circus, and during the show, the clowns paraded out the cutest string of French poodles that wore tutus and danced about. One of the poodles, a frisky vixen named "Brigitte," strayed from the clowns, ignored the calls of her trainer, and jumped right at mom. Quicker than you could say, "Voila!," Brigitte emptied the entirety of her bowels upon mom's lap. The crowd erupted in laughter. Mom was mortified.

Mom sued the circus, the clowns, the trainer, and the breeder who brought Brigitte into this world. Mom also sued Brigitte's parents, but they were thrown out of the lawsuit on a summary judgment application because of their inability to adequately respond to the allegations.

Mom demanded compensation for all of her pain and suffering, as well as for the great public humiliation she suffered. "That bitch stole my son's sixth birthday," cried mom. "I can never get it back."

Mom got no money for her suffering, but she did, as part of her settlement, receive a voucher for two free circus tickets—not in the first row—every year for the rest of her life.

☀ LIFE LESSON:
... but it ain't always bad.

EPILOGUE

This book began with a simple question, "What does a lawyer know about life?" And it quipped a simple response, "On most days, not much." But why is that? What is it about the way that lawyers act and think that makes people believe we don't know or care about life? And are we wrongly judged? After all, lawyers have very hard jobs. Most of us work day and night, most of us have faith in a greater good, and most of us at some point in our career have championed causes that no one else would or could because we honestly believe in a system that values every person and every cause—even those people and causes that are not popular, or pretty, or prosperous. That's what lawyers do.

At the same time, the stories in this book also make me wonder, what is it about society that encourages and rewards lawyers to act in ways that could be seen as not knowing or caring about life? Think about it. The same qualities that most people hate about lawyers (aggression, posturing, zeal) are the very same qualities that people seek when hiring a lawyer to represent themselves.

So many parents tell their children, "You should be a lawyer when you grow up." Yet, those same parents can be heard at dinner parties and cocktail hours telling lawyer jokes, talking to their friends about how to avoid jury duty, and bashing the legal system. Lawyers are the only professionals I know who all at the same time are desperately needed, highly regarded, and deeply despised. It's no wonder that, every once in a while, we act less than human or we forget that we care. Sometimes we have to, just to survive.

Lawyers know more about life than people give us credit for. Believe it or not, every lawyer I know started his or her life as an actual human being. However, good lawyers often have to put human emotions aside in order to get the job done. Thankfully, though, there also are many great lawyers who dare to bring the emotions back in.

While reading this book, there may have come a moment when you said to yourself, "No way. That could never happen." Or maybe you thought, "Are people really that stupid?"

Some of these stories I did see for myself. Some are war stories from colleagues; and yes, some of these cases are pure legend. But does it really matter?

If you learned one thing, if you saw the legal system a little differently, if you experienced the world in a new way for just a few fleeting seconds, then this book has done its job.

Keep living, keep asking questions, and keep looking for lessons to be learned.

BOOK CLUB QUESTIONS

• One goal of the book is to elicit strong feelings. Another goal is to show the humanity of lawyers and others who work in the justice system. Did the book achieve either of those goals?

• What chapter or story did you find the most surprising? Were you surprised by what happened to the litigants, or to the lawyers, or to the judges, or to the other people in the story?

• Do you think this book made you see lawyers and the law in a different way? If so, how?

• Why do you think so many people are afraid of the law or don't understand how the legal system works?

• Would you ever want to be a judge? How would you feel about having to preside over a murder trial, or having to decide who gets custody, or even having to determine the more mundane things like whether someone should pay his traffic ticket?

• Do you agree with the author's definition of what it means to be a professional? Is there a better definition that you would give? Has there ever been a time when you had to keep plugging along, "even when it sucked"?

• If you could offer some life lessons to a lawyer, what would you convey?

• In the chapter entitled "Quench that Thirst," there is a section about the importance of having a vice. Do you agree that every professional (and every person) should have some type of personal vice? Is there a particular vice that helps you get through the day?

• If you could meet any character in the book and have a conversation with him or her, who would you want to meet, and what would you want to say or ask? Is there a character or story that you would want to learn more about? What else would you want to know?

• The end of the book tells us that "Shit Happens." Have you ever had "Shit Happen" to you that looked really bad at first, but then it turned out to be good for you in the long run? When and how did you start to realize that things weren't as bad as you initially thought? What did you learn in the process?